MW01222400

sexy
laundry

sexy laundry

a play by Michele Riml

Playwrights Canada Press
Toronto ° Canada

PLAYWRIGHTS CANADA PRESS
The Canadian Drama Publisher
215 Spadina Ave., Suite 230, Toronto, Ontario, Canada, M5T 2C7
phone 416.703.0013   fax 416.408.3402
orders@playwrightscanada.com • www.playwrightscanada.com

The publisher acknowledges the support of the Canadian taxpayers through the Government of Canada Book Publishing Industry Development Program, the Canada Council for the Arts, the Ontario Arts Council, and the Ontario Media Development Corporation.

Front cover image and design: Bryan Jay Ibeas
Production Editor: MZK

LIBRARY AND ARCHIVES CANADA CATALOGUING IN PUBLICATION

Riml, Michele
Sexy laundry / Michele Riml.

A play.
ISBN 978-0-88754-811-6

I. Title.

PS8635.I555S49 2009   C812'.6   C2008-907479-3

First edition: February 2009.
Printed and bound by Canadian Printco Ltd. at Scarborough, Canada.

Sexy Laundry is dedicated to my beloved husband Michael St. John Smith, who teaches me every day how to have a loving and true marriage.

Acknowledgements / Playwright's Notes

Sexy Laundry would not exist without the formidable talent, faith and friendship of director Andrew McIlroy.

I would also like to acknowledge Bill Millerd and Rachel Ditor of the Arts Club Theatre Company in Vancouver for workshopping and championing the play; Roy Surette at the Belfry Theatre for giving *Sexy Laundry* its first professional production; Allan Morgan, Meredith Bain Woodward, Susinn McFarlen and Kevin McNulty for breathing first life into Henry and Alice; Colette Riml for her constat and unconditional love and support; and Barb and Don McCandlish, married for an inspirational forty-seven years and still counting.

Sexy Laundry was first performed at the 2002 Vancouver Fringe Festival with the following company:

HENRY	Allan Morgan
ALICE	Meredith Bain Woodward
Director	Andrew McIlroy

After workshopping the play through the Arts Club Theatre ReACT reading series, *Sexy Laundry* was produce in 2003 at the Belfry Theatre in Victoria and in the fall of 2003 at the Arts Club Theatre with the following company:

HENRY	Allan Morgan
ALICE	Susinn McFarlane
Director	Andrew McIlroy
Artistic director	Roy Surette
Stage manager	Timothy O'Gorman
Lighting designer	Rebekah Johnson
Associate designer	Shawn Derksen
Costume and set designer	Andrew McIlroy

2 / Michele Riml

Characters

ALICE Lane   fiftysomething
HENRY Lane   fiftysomething

Setting

The play takes place in room 219 at the L Hotel or Haute'L, an extremely chic, somewhat uncomfortable hotel. The bathroom is offstage.

Two-Act Version of Sexy Laundry

Sexy Laundry was written as a one-act play, and that is the author's preferred version. The play, however, has been successfully produced in two-acts. In the case of staging the play in two acts, the first act breaks on page 36 and follows as indicated below.

ALICE   But you know, all I could think of at that point was one thing... one overriding thought... you know what that thought was, Henry? *(pause)* I should get a divorce.

HENRY   *(disbelieving)* What?

        Lights out. End of act one.

Act Two picks up with ALICE and HENRY in the same spot.

        HENRY repeats his last line.

HENRY   *(disbelieving)* What?

ALICE   I just saw it so clearly, Henry. What I've become. What we've become.

The play continues as written.

*Open on HENRY and ALICE in a hotel room at the
L Hotel. The L (or the Haut'L) is ridiculously chic. The
bed floats on a pedestal in the middle of the room, awash
in expensive sheets and pillows. ALICE Lane lies on the
bed. Underneath the sheets HENRY Lane kneads
ALICE's buttocks like he's working a loaf of bread.
ALICE indulges the massage as long as she can. She
puts on her reading glasses and flips through
a handbook—Sex for Dummies.*

ALICE   Henry? Henry! My bum is relaxed already.

HENRY   What?

ALICE   You're not making bread. You're supposed to be giving
me a massage.

HENRY pokes his head out from the sheets.

HENRY   I am giving you a massage. Doesn't it feel good?

ALICE   It feels fine, but unlike my shoulders and back and feet
even, my bum is incredibly tension-free.

HENRY   That's cause I am a good masseur.

ALICE   No. That's because I have a relaxed ass. Can you do my
shoulders?

HENRY   You're telling me how to give you a massage.

ALICE   I'm sharing my needs with you.

HENRY   You're bossing me around.

ALICE   The book says to share.

HENRY   The book says to explore, too. I'm exploring your ass.

ALICE   Well strike out to new territory.

HENRY jabs reluctantly at ALICE's shoulders.

HENRY   How is this supposed to get me in the mood?

ALICE   It's supposed to relax me and free us of our inhibitions.

HENRY   It hurts my thumbs.

ALICE   Don't push so hard.

HENRY   Don't tell me how to do it.

ALICE   Well if you'd listen the first time I wouldn't have to tell you.

> *HENRY massages while ALICE groans. He slaps her butt.*

HENRY   There. Are you relaxed?

ALICE   Sort of, I guess.

HENRY   Good, my turn.

> *HENRY flops down on his stomach beside ALICE.*

ALICE   What? No way!

HENRY   What do you mean, no way? I did you. Now you have to do me.

ALICE   Not on the same day.

HENRY   Not on the same day?

ALICE   I'm relaxed now. It will make me tense to give you a massage. It's your turn tomorrow.

HENRY   You want me to be relaxed tomorrow. We're supposed to both be relaxed to lose our inhibitions. We're not just losing your inhibitions.

ALICE   You're supposed to enjoy exploring my body.

HENRY   I did. Now you can enjoy exploring mine.

ALICE   It's not relaxing to give someone a massage.

> *ALICE begins to reluctantly massage HENRY.*

HENRY   Tell me about it.

ALICE   So it didn't turn you on to massage me?

HENRY   Well sort of, I guess, but it's a lot of work.

ALICE   You used to love it.

HENRY   Well I guess there's more to explore today.

ALICE   WHAT!

HENRY   I'm kidding. I just mean, the New World was discovered a long time ago. Now it's more like going to the same time-share.

ALICE   You know there's one thing you're worse at than giving a massage. Metaphor. You don't know how to make a metaphor, Henry.

HENRY   So?

ALICE   So, metaphor takes imagination. That's why we're here.

HENRY   To make metaphors.

ALICE   To spice things up. To use our imaginations.

HENRY   I thought we were here to get laid.

ALICE   Very nice.

HENRY   Look, I came on this weekend because you asked me to. Because things have gotten stale, as you say. I'm doing the exercises the best I can. But no one told me I'd have to write an English exam. You married an engineer, Alice, not a poet.

ALICE   Well Henry, there is no English exam. But sex is communication. So maybe language is an appropriate metaphor for a sexual encounter.

HENRY   You are so sexy when you talk like this.

          ALICE gets off the bed, wrapping her robe around her.

ALICE   I'm not trying to be sexy, Henry.

HENRY   I know.

ALICE   Oh great. So you don't think I'm sexy. Now it's my fault.

HENRY   Your fault for what?

ALICE   That we don't have sex.

HENRY We have sex.

ALICE When? When was the last time we had sex? You can't remember, can you?

HENRY Sure, I can remember. I don't count like you do, Alice. We do it when we do it.

ALICE Well we don't do it much anymore.

HENRY Well maybe we don't, so?

ALICE So? So! You don't think that's significant, Henry? That doesn't say something about us? About our relationship? About our marriage?

HENRY We're busy people.

ALICE We're just not finding the time. Is that it?

HENRY You know what my job's been like lately. Somebody has to pick up the slack.

ALICE I've been picking up the slack of raising three children and managing a career for twenty-five years.

> *ALICE begins to make the bed, swatting HENRY away when he attempts to help her.*

HENRY So you're busy too.

ALICE But I'm not too busy to want to connect with my husband when he gets home.

HENRY We connect.

ALICE How? By you coming in the door and dropping your coat on the chair and turning on the TV?

HENRY I like to unwind when I get home.

ALICE Well I like to unwind too. After dinner is made and the dishes are done and Jason's in his room and I've returned all my email and reheated your dinner, which you never eat with the family anymore, I too, Henry, like to unwind. And I'd like to unwind with my husband.

HENRY · So you don't want me to do the one thing I enjoy. Which is to watch the news for an hour when I get home.

ALICE · I don't mind if you watch the news. I just want to connect with you.

HENRY · So sit with me.

ALICE · I don't find CNN or *20/20* or the latest report on the hell the world's going to—to be particularly relaxing.

HENRY · So you don't want me to watch it.

ALICE · I said I don't mind.

HENRY · Then what do you want?

> *ALICE finishes making the bed. She addresses HENRY sitting on the bed.*

ALICE · Well I'd like to cuddle. Maybe give each other a foot massage.

HENRY · Oh God.

ALICE · What's wrong with that?

HENRY · Alice, I'm sorry, but honestly the last thing I want to do after being on my feet all day is rub yours.

ALICE · You sit behind a desk, Henry.

HENRY · It's an expression, Alice. You see my point.

ALICE · Perhaps I would massage your feet.

HENRY · When, Alice? When have you ever said the word massage in reference to giving rather than receiving—when?

ALICE · Well maybe if we could just cuddle.

HENRY · While I'm watching the news.

ALICE · We could cuddle on the couch.

HENRY · And then you would talk to me.

ALICE · I might.

HENRY   So you would like to cuddle and talk on the couch while I'm watching the news.

> *ALICE snuggles up to HENRY on the bed, her head on his shoulder.*

ALICE   Yes.

HENRY   And then see where that leads...

ALICE   Possibly.

HENRY   So possibly we would be cuddling, talking and having sex on the couch while I'm watching the news. That's a lot to do while I'm watching the news.

ALICE   Well you don't have to watch the news.

> *HENRY leaps off the bed. ALICE falls into the pillows.*

HENRY   And there it is. You see! You don't want me to watch the news.

ALICE   I'm just saying if something more interesting comes up, surely we can turn off the TV!

HENRY   Now the TV's off.

ALICE   Don't you think having sex with me is more interesting than watching TV?

HENRY   Must I relinquish one pleasure to have another? Could I not, in this godforsaken world, have both?

ALICE   You're the one who said we don't have any time.

HENRY   We can make time.

ALICE   When, during commercials?

> *HENRY paces around the room, exasperated.*

HENRY   We're here, aren't we?

ALICE   What?

HENRY   Here we are making time. Making time to make love. But are we making love? No. What are we making, Alice? Is this love we're making?

ALICE   No.

HENRY   No. You are making me mad. I am making you mad. We are not making love. We are making mad.

ALICE   I'm not mad, Henry.

HENRY   What are you then?

ALICE   I'm sad.

>*Pause.*

HENRY   Why do you do that?

ALICE   What?

HENRY   Why do you always say you're sad when you *are* mad?

ALICE   I am sad. I'm sad for us.

HENRY   You are not sad for us. You are mad at me.

ALICE   No I'm not. I'm sad for us. I'm sad that we've lost something and we don't know how to find it.

HENRY   You are mad at me because I come home late and watch the news and don't help enough with the kids and the house. Admit it.

ALICE   No, I'm not. I'm sad for what we've lost.

HENRY   Oh poor, suffering Alice is sad for us, while old, selfish Henry is just mad at poor Alice. How did you get to be so good, Alice?

ALICE   Now you're just being mean, Henry.

>*HENRY sits in one of the uncomfortable L chairs.*

HENRY   Mean, mad, selfish Henry. Why would you want to be here with me in the first place?

ALICE   To reconnect. To try and find what we had.

HENRY   Well we're not going to find it if you're always right and I'm always wrong.

ALICE   That's true.

HENRY   Don't agree with me.

ALICE   All right.

HENRY   Alice!

ALICE   Henry!

HENRY   Give me the book.

> *HENRY and ALICE sit on the bed with* Sex for Dummies. *HENRY takes ALICE's reading glasses and puts them on his nose. He peruses the book. ALICE waits as long as she can and then grabs the book and the glasses from him.*

ALICE   I've marked some really good ones. Look, here's an easy one… personalizing your private parts.

HENRY   Jesus Christ.

ALICE   *(reads)* "Lovers often give each other nicknames to facilitate closeness and add sparkle to sex talk. Try using your lover's private pet name at a dinner party to titillate your lover."

HENRY   What the hell?

ALICE   "For example… if you've called your partner's joy box—"

> *ALICE gets stuck on the word joy box. She and HENRY look at each other and then she skips to the appendix. Not finding the word there, she skips back to the exercise.*

I guess that's a woman's… you know. I don't know. I skipped the introduction. "If you've called your wife's joy box Wonder Woman—work Wonder Woman into the conversation. Example: 'Does anybody remember the last time they saw a Wonder Woman cartoon?' Or, 'Wonder Woman is fabulous, isn't she?' You and your partner can share a secret sexy moment anywhere with your pet names. Use them often."

HENRY   They've got to be kidding. Would Wonder Woman pass the cream corn? Come on.

ALICE   I like the idea. Give me a name.

HENRY   You have a name. It's Alice.

ALICE   Henry, we both have to participate if this is going to work.

HENRY   It's asinine. I'm not going to use your "name" at a dinner party or any other place.

ALICE   Okay, I'll give you a name.

HENRY   I don't want a name.

ALICE   I just have to think.

> *HENRY paces around the room. He stops and sniffs at an aromatherapy pot perched on a stand.*

HENRY   What is this stuff again?

ALICE   It's aromatherapy. Arabian Dreams. For ambience.

HENRY   Why does this room have to smell like a Third World country?

ALICE   Henry! It's nice. It creates an atmosphere.

HENRY   An atmosphere of—

ALICE   *(interrupting)* Frank.

HENRY   What?

ALICE   That's what I'll call "you."

HENRY   Frank. What the hell kind of name is that?

ALICE   It's a perfect name. It works on different levels.

HENRY   Frank?

ALICE   Frank. As in lay it on the line. Straightforward. Upright.

> *HENRY plops into another chair, unconsciously placing a pillow over his private parts.*

HENRY   Couldn't you think of something a little more?...

ALICE   Frank as in franks and beans.

HENRY   Alice.

ALICE   Frank as in "Frankly my dear, I don't give a damn."

HENRY   I don't like Frank.

ALICE lifts up the pillow and whispers.

ALICE   Shh, don't tell Frank that.

HENRY   Alice, be serious. Frank doesn't work.

ALICE runs her hand up HENRY's leg.

ALICE   Oh, Frank just needs a little help getting started.

HENRY   Alice!

HENRY jumps off the chair to get away from ALICE.

ALICE   Well what would you call it?

HENRY   Not Frank.

ALICE   Well give me a name. Otherwise it's Frank. You agreed to do some of these exercises, Henry.

Pause.

HENRY   *(mumbles)* Caesar.

ALICE   What?

HENRY   Caesar.

ALICE   Caesar?

HENRY   Caesar.

ALICE laughs.

ALICE   That's what you want me to call it—you?

HENRY   I don't want you to call it anything. But for the purpose of ending this ridiculous exercise I choose Caesar.

ALICE bows.

ALICE   Hail Caesar.

HENRY   Exactly.

ALICE   Oh my God, Henry.

HENRY   Give me the book. I'm picking.

ALICE   Certainly, Caesar.

HENRY   Alice…

ALICE   I'll have a Caesar with no croutons.

HENRY rifles through the book.

HENRY   Jesus, where did you get this thing?

ALICE   At the library.

HENRY   They keep stuff like this at the library?

ALICE   They have many different books at the library.

HENRY   You checked it out.

ALICE   No, I hid it in my bag, ran through the turnstiles and when the alarm went off two security guards grabbed me. I had to shoot one to get away. Give it to me. *(ALICE grabs the book.)* Okay. Here's one. "Fantasy Share. Let your partner's imagination flame the fires of passion. Lie back, relax and get ready for sparks to fly as you each whisper your most intimate fantasy to one another." Okay?

HENRY   Okay. *(pause)* You go first.

ALICE   Why do I have to go first?

HENRY   Ladies first.

ALICE   I'd rather listen.

HENRY   I have to think about it for a minute. You start.

ALICE   Why, you don't have fantasies?

HENRY   I've got to find one I can say out loud.

ALICE   Well so do I.

HENRY   It was your idea to come here. You start.

ALICE   Okay, I just have to think…

> *ALICE walks around the room preparing herself. She ends up at a chair, which becomes her seat in the coffee shop. As ALICE reveals her fantasy she becomes increasingly, emotionally, but not sexually, involved in it, seeing the man in the coffee shop, blushing and covering her eyes when he reveals himself. As she speaks, HENRY, sitting on the bed, becomes more and more tightly wound.*

Okay. Here it goes. Don't laugh. I'm sitting in a coffee shop. I'm wearing a black leather skirt and black leather boots, a silky white blouse with no bra. I'm a size eight. What the hell, it's my fantasy. I'm a six. I order a coffee from a very handsome Italian waiter. He brings me the coffee and puts his hand on my shoulder. He whispers… "You are so beautiful," but he says it in Italian. *(She repeats the line in English with an Italian accent.)* "You are so beautiful." As he puts the coffee down I catch the eye of a man watching me. I turn away. The man approaches my table and sits down. I pretend not to see him. I feel a hand on my thigh. I look up and see the waiter putting the closed sign on the door. And then he takes off his apron and I notice that he isn't wearing anything underneath it. He comes over to the table. He asks me if I would like another coffee. I say no. *(surprised)* Then he bends down and kisses the man sitting beside me—

HENRY   What the?

ALICE   It's my fantasy, Henry. And then they turn to me and I know what they want. And I smile. And they help me with my clothes. I sweep the coffee from the table. And then… *(ALICE searches for the words, not quite able to get graphic with the fantasy.)* we're together… and… well… you know the rest. Henry?

> *By this time HENRY has his head between his knees.*

HENRY   Yes?

ALICE   What is it? Do you want me to fill in more of the details?

HENRY   No. No. I get it. That's fine. Fine.

ALICE   Was it sexy?

HENRY   Sexy. Very sexy.

ALICE   What then?

HENRY   Well, couldn't you just have a regular fantasy. You know, a field of flowers, a white knight or maybe a kind of *From Here To Eternity* waves crashing sort of thing.

ALICE   I think you've confused sexual fantasy with a maxi-pad commercial.

HENRY   Well excuse me if I'm a little surprised that my wife wants to have an affair over espresso with a gay Italian waiter and some guy she's never met!

ALICE   It's a fantasy, Henry. It's not an affair.

HENRY   What if someone came in?

ALICE   Came in?

>*HENRY gestures to the "shop."*

HENRY   To the shop while you were…

>*ALICE gestures to the "sign."*

ALICE   The sign is on the door.

HENRY   If they ignored the sign.

ALICE   Well I suppose they could join in too.

HENRY   So now you're in a goddamn orgy.

ALICE   It's not real, Henry.

HENRY   But this is what you think about?

ALICE   Maybe. If I'm thinking like that.

HENRY   Well how am I supposed to compete with that?

ALICE   Compete? You're not. You don't have to compete with what's in my mind.

HENRY   Hah!

ALICE   What?

HENRY   I don't have to compete with what's in your mind?

ALICE   No, you don't.

HENRY   Yes I do, Alice. It's always what's in your mind or on your mind that gets us in trouble.

ALICE   What do you mean?

HENRY   Nothing ever measures up to what's in your mind, Alice. And that includes me.

ALICE   That's not true, Henry.

HENRY   Yes it is, Alice. You have so many ideas about the way things are supposed to be. I'm supposed to be. You have ideas about how I should hang the towels—two folds, not one—make the bed—one fold, not two. How long I should watch TV for. What I wear. How much I should eat and not eat. You even have an idea about how I should chew. Ten times and then swallow. Conversation between every bite. I'm supposed to be strong but romantic. Supportive but not controlling. Telepathic. Omniscient. Send you flowers and take you dancing.

ALICE   What's wrong with flowers?

HENRY   Nothing. When they come from me. When I'm not being sent icy telepathic send-me-flower vibes from you.

ALICE   If I don't tell you, you won't do it.

HENRY   How do you know that?

ALICE   Because you don't.

HENRY   I might. If I had half a chance to think about it. Besides, I can't dance. And maybe flowers aren't my thing.

ALICE   You don't even try to dance. And maybe flowers are my thing.

HENRY   Well I don't see the…

ALICE   Oh God, don't say it, Henry.

HENRY   You spend fifty bucks and then they just die.

ALICE   Well I've spent twenty-five years with you and you're just going to die too, but I still like having you around!

HENRY puts his hand on ALICE's shoulder.

HENRY   I sent you flowers on your birthday.

ALICE   I know. But it's nice when they're not expected. You know…

HENRY   I know. I know. It's the thought. It's the gesture. It's that I'm thinking of you.

ALICE   You do think of me still, don't you Henry?

HENRY   Of course I think of you.

ALICE   In that way?

HENRY   In what way?

ALICE   In a sexy way. Do you think I'm sexy?

HENRY   Sure. I mean, I'm not the one thinking about some Italian looking to dip his biscotti in someone else's cappuccino.

ALICE   So what do you think about?

HENRY   About you?

ALICE   About me. About you. About the dog… I don't care. What gets you going, Henry? Because I don't know anymore. Leather, heels, whips, chains? Do you think about that stuff?

HENRY   Sure, sure, I'm a man.

ALICE   Okay, then share your fantasy.

HENRY   I don't like this exercise.

ALICE   I did mine. You promised to participate.

HENRY   Oh for God's sake.

ALICE   Just close your eyes and share what comes up.

HENRY   I don't want to close my eyes.

ALICE   Fine, whatever. Here, I'll lie here and close mine.

HENRY   Okay.

> *As ALICE prepares herself on the bed HENRY motions for her to cover her eyes. ALICE dutifully places her hands over her eyes. HENRY steps into his own spotlight. He is in his world. ALICE remains on the bed as time stops for a moment.*

My fantasy. My fantasy by Henry Lane. I come home from a long day at the office. My office. My corner office with a view. A view of the new Lane Towers. I'm coming home from a long day at the office. Rich, a young guy, stops me before I get on the elevator. Says he needs a little Lane insight. I give him a few minutes. Show him a different way to go. It helps. It's nothing. He shakes my hand. I come home from a long but challenging and financially rewarding day at the office. The lights on the porch are on, welcoming me into my warm but not overheated home. My wife greets me at the door with a smile. There is no concern, worry, anger, rage, disappointment, sadness or reluctance on her face. She kisses my cheek, takes my coat and offers me a drink. She switches on the news for me. My Ivy League college attending daughter brings me my slippers. I notice that her clothes cover all parts of her abdomen and buttocks. At the dinner table I tell a story and my children laugh. They think I'm funny and wise. I reprimand my young son, gently but firmly, for his elbows on the table. My wife smiles and nods in appreciation. We know how lucky we are. The kids do the dishes. My wife speaks gaily about her day... her charity work at the non-denominational church we attend regularly, the large commission she's earned from her latest real estate deal, a part-time job she holds for the sheer love of it, not because things are tight and we need the extra income. She asks my opinion about the decor in the living room. I understand what she's talking about. I give a sage answer about sisal carpet that pleases her into giving me a back rub. With no expectations. We curl up in bed together, each with a good book. We read, content in our shared silence...

ALICE Henry? Henry... do you have one yet?

Lights down on HENRY's space. He steps back into the room with ALICE.

HENRY What?

ALICE Have you thought of a fantasy?

HENRY I don't know.

ALICE Just start with where you are.

HENRY sits on the bed. He looks around the room for cues to his fantasy.

HENRY Uh, I'm sitting in a room.

ALICE A room?

HENRY A room. I'm sitting on a bed.

ALICE What kind of room?

HENRY A room with a bed. A bedroom.

ALICE Is it our bedroom? Describe it.

HENRY No. It's a hotel bedroom. I'm sitting on a bed in a hotel room.

ALICE And...

HENRY walks over to the door.

HENRY And... and the door opens...

ALICE What are you wearing?

HENRY   I'm wearing a bathrobe and pyjamas. Are you going to let me do this?

ALICE   Okay. The door opens…

HENRY   The door opens and… *(HENRY picks up the room service card by the phone.)* the maid comes in. And she's gorgeous.

ALICE   Gorgeous?

HENRY   Yeah, the gorgeous maid comes into the room—

ALICE   Gorgeous is pretty descriptive.

HENRY   Yeah, well—

ALICE   You can't describe the room, but all of a sudden the imaginary maid is gorgeous.

HENRY   Do you want me to stop?

ALICE   What's she wearing?

HENRY   What? She's wearing a maid's uniform.

ALICE   Is that all?

HENRY   Ah, she has on high heels? A leather apron.

ALICE   Oh. So she's not really the maid.

HENRY   *(a little taken aback)* Who is she?

ALICE   I don't know. A gorgeous woman in a maid's uniform. It's your fantasy.

HENRY   So she comes in and… God, I don't know…

ALICE   What does she say?

HENRY   *(reads from the room service card)* Ah, if you'd like turndown service press… press me hard, Henry.

ALICE   Oh, and she knows your name. What do you say?

HENRY   They charge for that.

ALICE   What?

HENRY   They actually have a turndown service fee.

ALICE   A fee?

HENRY shows ALICE the room service card.

HENRY   Where did you find this place?

ALICE   Henry, what happened to the maid?

HENRY   I don't know. She's waiting for a goddamn tip like everyone else in this hotel.

ALICE sits up on the bed.

ALICE   Henry, you're not even trying.

HENRY   What is this place called again? The P?

ALICE   The L.

HENRY   What does the L stand for?

ALICE   It doesn't stand for anything. It's just the L.

HENRY   It stands for ludicrous.

ALICE   The L is the hottest new hotel in the city. It's a synthesis of Eastern design and Western sensibility. It's the place to try.

HENRY   Where did you read that gobbledygook?

ALICE   *Vancouver Magazine.* *

HENRY   Of course.

ALICE   It's new. It's different and I wanted to try it. Are we going to do this or not?

HENRY   All right. Look, I'm fine with having sex, but I'll tell you one thing: Talking about it is not my thing.

ALICE   Okay, here. You pick something.

ALICE tosses HENRY the book. HENRY flips through it as he speaks.

HENRY   You are so taken in by fluff, Alice. Solid engineering is what holds this building up. Not the reviews.

---

* The magazine should reflect the city in which the production is taking place.

ALICE   I know that. An engineer worked on this building too, Henry.

HENRY   Yeah, and where's his name in the review? I bet they give more credit to the guy who designed the napkins.

ALICE   Without the reviews no one would come.

HENRY   And that would be a tragedy. No one paying fifteen times the average price for a phone call or a cup of coffee.

ALICE   There's nothing wrong with trying something new.

HENRY   All right. Here's another one. Double Blind.

ALICE   Read it to me.

HENRY   *(reads)* "The purpose of this exercise is to use all your senses other than sight in a meaningful exploration of your partner's body. Explore with touch, taste and smell to feel your partner's body—" I can't read this stuff out loud. What we do is blindfold each other. We're not allowed to talk. We just kind of see what happens as we… explore.

ALICE   Okay. Sure.

HENRY   No talking allowed.

ALICE   Okay.

HENRY   Okay, then we need blindfolds.

ALICE   Right, uh…

HENRY   I'll check the bathroom. Where is the bathroom?

            HENRY goes offstage. ALICE smoothes the comforter on the bed and checks herself in the mirror. She sucks in her tummy, turning this way and that, not entirely pleased with what she sees. She opens her robe a little. She dabs some perfume on her wrists, neck. Considers herself in the mirror and then applies some perfume to the back of her knees too. When she can't get quite the look she wants in front of the mirror she tries to position herself in a flattering way on the bed. She strikes a pose of the wanton woman but then can't see herself in the mirror. She stretches to see herself in the mirror and maintain the pose. She uses the sheet to disguise her "flawed" areas. Just as she has a pose she can live with, HENRY calls out.

How much did we pay for this room?

ALICE jumps from the bed, pulling the robe tightly around her, throwing the bed together. She perches primly on the end of the bed.

ALICE   You know how much we paid.

HENRY returns with a towel in hand.

HENRY   Three hundred dollars and the towels are as thin as sheets.

ALICE   Will they work as blindfolds?

HENRY   They won't even work as towels.

ALICE   What about a pillowcase?

HENRY   Look at these things! Doesn't anyone do anything right anymore?

ALICE   Here.

She tries to tie a pillowcase around HENRY's eyes.

HENRY   It's short-sighted. You invest in quality because quality pays in the end. In the end someone will not return to this hotel because of the quality of the towels. I'm going to give them a call.

ALICE   Henry, no! Who are you going to call?

HENRY   The manager of the hotel. The only reason they do this is because they think they can get away with it. They can scrimp on towels and no one will care. *(to the phone)* Hello, yes this is two nineteen. I'd like to speak to the manager. I have a complaint about the towels. Yes. Thank you. *(to ALICE)* They're putting me right through.

ALICE   Hold still.

HENRY   And the reverse is true as well. If the towels were of quality one might return because of that.

> *ALICE gives up on the pillowcase.*

ALICE   This isn't working.

HENRY   Nobody thinks about the long-run anymore.

ALICE   I had no idea you cared this much about towels.

HENRY   It's the little decisions that have the biggest ramifications.

ALICE   Do you really need to do this right now?

HENRY   Alice, these are the small battles you have to fight. *(to the phone)* Hello, who? Housekeeping? No, I wanted to talk to the manager. Yes, I do, about the towels. No, I don't need more towels. The towels I have are thin. Very thin. I don't want to write it on a customer satisfaction card. Put me back to the front desk.

ALICE   It's just a towel...

HENRY   A towel is not just a towel.

ALICE   ...Maybe something in my suitcase.

HENRY   It says something about how these people think about us.

ALICE   We could use my sweater and your shirt.

> *ALICE grabs her sweater and his shirt from their suitcases.*

HENRY   These people think A, we don't care or B, we won't notice. Either way it's insulting.

ALICE   It's a towel, Henry.

HENRY   I like to get what I pay for.

ALICE   I paid for the room, Henry.

HENRY   You know what I mean. *(to the phone)* Yes, this is two nineteen. Yes, this is about towels. The towels are thin. Very thin. And I want to register a—they're Italian. The towels are. Well that's interesting but not entirely comforting—they are not exactly plush. Microfibre? Look, I don't care if Leonardo da Vinci designed them himself—they're thin. I like a warm, cozy towel when I get out of the shower—not a scarf. The towel rack is heated. Of course I noticed that. I also noticed there are only two towels on the rack… under the sink; well I must have missed them. Fine, perhaps you might provide some literature about your towels in the future. The Thin Towels of Tuscany or something like that. Yes, it is a good idea. Goodbye. *(He hangs up.)* The towels are Italian.

ALICE   Are we going to do this?

HENRY   Yeah, okay.

> *She ties the shirt as a blindfold around HENRY.*

Ow, not too tight.

ALICE   Can you see?

HENRY   No, I'm wearing a blindfold.

ALICE   I mean can you see through the blindfold?

HENRY   No. Give me yours.

> *HENRY gropes for her. ALICE gives him a sweater and sits on the bed for him to tie it on her.*

What is this?

ALICE   It's my sweater.

HENRY   It's so soft.

ALICE   It's cashmere.

> *He pulls the blindfold tight around her neck.*

HENRY   Is it new?

ALICE   I got it on sale. You're choking me.

HENRY   How much was it?

ALICE   It was on sale. I saved $150.

HENRY   Is that tight enough?

ALICE   Ow. I can still see. Here…

> *ALICE moves the blindfold. They speak to one another with the blindfolds on.*

HENRY   You don't save money by spending money. Look at the world economy. It just isn't working.

ALICE   The world economy. It's a sweater, Henry. I wanted it so I bought it.

HENRY   Everything's instant gratification today. And you know what happens when one man gets instant gratification? Another man is told to wait a few years. His turn will come. It's a joke.

> *ALICE removes her blindfold.*

ALICE   Henry, you didn't get the partnership.

HENRY   Rich got it.

ALICE   Why didn't you tell me?

HENRY   With us five years. Ten years younger than me.

ALICE   Henry.

HENRY   It doesn't matter.

> *ALICE takes HENRY's blindfold off.*

ALICE   It does matter, honey. Why didn't you tell me?

HENRY   I don't know. I was counting on it. I expected it. It was just a matter of course. I've been with them for so long. I felt stupid.

ALICE   It's not fair.

HENRY   His ideas are not grounded in a conservative sensibility.

ALICE   Jack said that?

HENRY   He's willing to try new things.

ALICE   But you have the experience.

HENRY   Rich impresses them. He's got big ideas. He just came off the Atlas project. He looks at an old building and sees a new one in its place. I look at an old building and see something to work with. It's not exciting.

ALICE   Did you say anything to Jack?

HENRY   What's there to say? It all sounds like sour grapes.

ALICE   Well you've been there a long time and you will be rewarded for that. You have been. And ultimately it's a job, Henry. A job you do very well. But a job all the same.

HENRY   I know. I'm just sorry.

ALICE   Sorry? Henry, you have nothing to be sorry about. I know how hard you work.

HENRY   The money would have…

ALICE   (softly) We have plenty. We're lucky people.

HENRY   You're good about this stuff, Al.

ALICE   Come on, let's not let it ruin our weekend.

> HENRY moves to put his blindfold back on; ALICE takes his hand.

HENRY   Back to the blindfold?

ALICE   We don't have to. Why don't you tell me a fantasy. A real one this time.

HENRY   Oh, Alice…

ALICE   Shh, close your eyes. What do you see?

> ALICE rests her head on HENRY's shoulder, looking out at his fantasy. As she sees it she becomes increasingly uncomfortable.

HENRY   I see… I see a beach. A tropical beach. There's a girl on a blanket. She's laying out a picnic. She's wearing a dress over her swimsuit. The dress slips off her shoulder as she places the picnic on the blanket. She has very smooth skin. I can see the outline of her breasts through the fabric—

ALICE   Let's do the blindfold.

> *ALICE jumps off the bed.*

HENRY   What?

ALICE   I just... you're right. It's weird talking about this stuff.

HENRY   You didn't like my—

ALICE   No, no, I did. I just think the not talking thing is better. Please, Henry.

HENRY   Okay. All right. Let's do the blindfold.

ALICE   This will be fun.

> *ALICE and HENRY tie on their own blindfolds.*

HENRY   Whatever you say.

ALICE   We're not supposed to talk, right?

HENRY   Right. No talking.

> *ALICE knocks HENRY on the chin.*

Ow!

ALICE   Oh my God, Henry, did I hurt you?

HENRY   If your elbow connecting with my chin constitutes injury. Yes.

ALICE   I'm sorry, baby.

HENRY   Let's make our way to the bed where it's safer.

ALICE   Give me your hand.

> *ALICE puts her hand through HENRY's legs and waves it around.*

HENRY   Oh.

Susinn McFarlane and Allan Morgan
photo by: David Cooper

ALICE   Oh. Hello Caesar.

HENRY   Alice, give me your hand.

They shuffle toward the bed.

ALICE   Don't things seem farther away in the dark? *(She bangs her knee up against the bed.)* Ow!

HENRY   No.

ALICE   Found it.

HENRY   Okay, I am on the bed.

ALICE   I am on the bed.

HENRY   Hello.

ALICE   Hello.

HENRY   The sheets are thin too, eh?

ALICE   Henry.

HENRY   Sorry, come here.

ALICE grabs his butt.

ALICE   You have always had the nicest butt.

HENRY   No talking.

HENRY and ALICE explore each other's bodies on their knees, oohing and aahing as they go. HENRY concentrates his hands around ALICE'S stomach. ALICE freezes, trying to keep going with the exercise but not happy with HENRY'S area of exploration.

ALICE   Henry, what are you doing?

HENRY   Exploring.

ALICE   My stomach?

HENRY   Oh Alice, you've got a real handful here.

ALICE   What?

HENRY   I never noticed the skin around your waist.

ALICE   The skin?

             ALICE bites HENRY's shoulder.

HENRY   It's so soft. Ow!

             ALICE takes off her blindfold and HENRY follows suit.

ALICE   Why are you doing this?

HENRY   What are you doing? Did you just bite me?

ALICE   You're not even trying to be nice.

HENRY   Alice, what!?

ALICE   If you don't want to be with me that's one thing. But don't start making fun of the weight I've gained.

HENRY   Alice, what are you talking about? I wasn't. I was exploring.

ALICE   You were commenting on how fat I've become.

HENRY   I was not.

ALICE   "Oh Alice, what a handful you have here."

HENRY   They call them love handles for a reason, Alice. Am I bleeding?

ALICE   Henry, don't patronize me. I know I've let myself go in that area. I just thought my husband could get past it.

HENRY   I was never on it. I didn't have to get past it.

ALICE   Don't lie to me. I've felt how you put your arms around me. Running them down my back. Feeling with your hands. Trying to see how much fatter I am.

HENRY   What?

ALICE   I know why we hardly make love anymore.

HENRY   Alice… you are so wrong here.

ALICE   You can't stand to touch me.

HENRY   Alice, come—

ALICE   Well, I'll tell you something, Mr. Henry Lane, you are not a perfect specimen. Your waist is thicker than your chest. You are not and never have been six foot three. And have you checked your hairline recently? If you are going to judge me by appearance you should have a look in the mirror first.

HENRY   I don't have to sit here and listen to this.

ALICE   Why is it that a man can let himself go and still expect his wife to be attractive, and thin, and still be attracted to him?

HENRY   I don't want you to be thin.

ALICE   So you think I'm fat.

HENRY   I didn't say that. I said I don't want you to be thin.

ALICE   So you want me to be fat?

HENRY   No, no, no. You see, that is where you are making a ridiculous leap, Alice.

ALICE   Thin or fat? What leap, Henry?

HENRY   It isn't either / or.

ALICE   Just answer my question. What would you rather I be, thin or fat? And don't lie.

HENRY   You. I'd rather you be you.

ALICE   What does that mean?

HENRY   It means the way you are is fine with me.

ALICE   Fat.

HENRY   Alice. This is a no-win conversation.

ALICE   You just don't understand. You're lucky. You're a man. It's different for you. You get older and wiser and even more attractive in some ways. I get older.

HENRY   You don't really believe that.

ALICE   Look at it out there, Henry. The movies. The magazines. It's Julia Roberts with Nick Nolte, and Julia Roberts with Richard Gere, and Julia Roberts with Denzel Washington. The men are diverse. Old. Different. The women are always Julia Roberts... or Carmon Diaz.

HENRY   Cameron. *

ALICE   Hah, you do notice. Where are all the women my age?

HENRY   Susan Sarandon still does movies, doesn't she?

ALICE   That's because her tits are still good. And even then she plays nuns or cancer patients. They go from perfect twentysomething specimens to somebody's mother overnight. Where is the vital, passionate, sexy fifty-year-old?

HENRY   They're actresses, Alice. In movies.

ALICE   Well what about your fantasy? The girl on the beach. Why does she have to be a girl?

HENRY   Because she was a girl.

ALICE   The truth is women my age become invisible unless you're trying to sell us liposuction or life insurance. Then we're everywhere.

HENRY   Comparing your life to the movies just doesn't make sense. That's fantasy.

ALICE   Well maybe I want a little fantasy in my life. Maybe going to the movies every other week isn't enough. Maybe I need a little sweep-me-off-my-feet romance once in a while. A little surprise.

HENRY   (*hesitant*) Is this going to be about flowers? Because I thought we'd covered that.

ALICE   It's not about flowers. It's about feeling alive.

HENRY   Well of course you're alive.

ALICE   I don't feel that way sometimes.

> *HENRY sits down on the bed beside her. He reaches over and pinches her leg.*

Ow!

---

* The actors' names can be changed to reflect popular culture at the time, young women with older men.

HENRY   Alive.

ALICE   You don't understand.

HENRY   I guess not.

ALICE   The other day, Henry, I went back to the gym.

HENRY   Universal Fitness?

ALICE   Fitness Universe.

HENRY   Right.

ALICE   I just looked in the mirror and decided now or never, Alice. So I decided to go that afternoon, no excuses.

HENRY   And did you?

> *ALICE looks at herself in the hotel room mirror and then steps into her spotlight facing front. She gets on the treadmill, running and pumping her arms as she speaks, seeing the girls on either side of her, completely absorbed in the retelling of her story. HENRY listens to her from the bed.*

ALICE   Oh I went all right. Except when I got to the gym I realized that I'd forgotten my gym bag so I had to improvise. I had my runners and Jason left his soccer shorts in the car so I took those in. I got on the treadmill in the ladies—only section. You know there's a mirror in the ladies section right in front of you. I started running, and I felt all right, like hey I haven't forgotten how to run. I'm not dead yet. Then this woman, this girl, this really beautiful girl got on the treadmill beside me. Twenty-two or twenty-three years old with long black hair swept up in a ponytail. She was wearing one of those little bra tops and the stripe on her Nikes matched the band in her hair. She got on the treadmill and she punched a few buttons. You know how those little lights come on for level one and level two all the way up to level twenty. Well she was at fifteen at least, with all sorts of hills and valleys. And she watched herself while she ran. My screen was at level one—my little dots were flatlining, just one even row of little red lights, no bumps or curves, just flatlining, like I was dead. So I bumped them up a couple of levels and I ran. I ran fast. And I made a decision to change my hair. Soon. Then another girl got on the treadmill on the other side of me. And she was all hills and valleys. Blonde with a diamond in her belly button. So I ramped up my treadmill a little more. The brunette started to pump her arms. I pumped mine. The blonde swung her hair over her shoulder. I swung mine. We ran fast, strong. The brunette smiled at me. I smiled back. The blonde upped her levels. I upped mine. I watched my little red dots peaking and falling in beautiful curves. I felt my heart beating and my lungs bursting. We ran together. Champions of the treadmill. Goddesses of Fitness Universe. Sisters in a marathon of, well, sisterhood. I saw the three of us in the mirror. We looked like the opening to *Charlie's Angels* when the angels are running together, hair flying, breasts bouncing. It was Farrah on one side and Jaclyn on the other, but instead of Kate in the middle they'd thrown in... Bosley. Two angels and me, Bosley. Bosley in Jason's soccer shorts. Bosley with frizzy hair. Bosley wearing a Jambalaya Mama T-shirt with spaghetti stains. Just then Jaclyn pulled the band out of her hair and it flew out behind her, and I swear to God she was moving in slow motion when she turned to me, speaking ever so slowly, and I looked down to where she was pointing, but it's hard to look down when you're running so fast and pumping your arms, and just as I saw that my shoelace was undone... I began to fly... *(ALICE throws her arms in the air.)* like an angel, Henry... I flew off the treadmill and through the air... and I hit the back wall. *(The lights come up again.)* And then there were only two angels, and me crashed against the back wall, Jason's soccer shorts split up the middle. And I looked up, Henry, to heaven, or God knows what, for something, and you know what I saw? ME. They have a mirror on the ceiling! The girls were very nice. They helped me up. They covered me with a towel. But you know, all I could think of at that point was one thing… one overriding thought… you know what that thought was, Henry? *(pause)* I should get a divorce.

HENRY   *(disbelieving)* What?

ALICE   I just saw it so clearly, Henry. What I've become. What we've become.

HENRY   You hit your head, Alice.

ALICE   I cleared my head.

HENRY   You brought me here to tell me that you want a divorce?

ALICE   I brought you here to see what's left of us.

HENRY   What's left of us is us.

ALICE   I don't know if that's enough.

HENRY   Enough? It is what it is.

ALICE   And what is that?

HENRY   It's us. Henry and Alice, married twenty-five years. Three kids. A house in a good neighbourhood. Nice friends. Is this some kind of test, Alice? Twenty-five years up against two days. If we don't have sex here we get a divorce? Are we really talking about this?

ALICE   I guess.

HENRY   *(really angry)* You guess. Jesus Christ. Divorce is not a word you just throw around. That crosses the line, Alice. You think because you're looking at yourself that gives you the right to cross all these lines. Everything is so goddamn disposable.

ALICE   I just want things to be as good as they could be.

HENRY   Look around, Alice. Look around. Nothing is as good as it could be. Nothing turns out exactly as we want it to. That's life. Maturity is accepting that. You make the best of it.

ALICE   We used to make dinner together.

HENRY   I help cook!

ALICE   Let me finish—we used to cook together. Now you chop and I stir. We're in the same room, that's all. I don't want to go along because we've been going along.

HENRY   We have a marriage. That's not just going along.

ALICE   So we have a marriage. Lots of people have that.

HENRY   Lots of people do not have what we have. Lots of people want what we have.

ALICE   Right.

HENRY   You don't just get what we have, Alice. You can't buy this. We had to build it. And it took twenty-five years. It took part-time jobs and two university degrees and one rental apartment after another and our first house and three children and your scare with breast cancer and my goddamn back and too many goddamn get-togethers with your family and getting up every day and going to bed everyday—together. That's us. The foundation. The walls. The bricks. The mortar. The roof. You may not like the facade. But that's us. And it's got to be worth something.

ALICE   I'm not talking about our history, Henry. I'm talking about how we feel about each other. Why it feels different. Why you're different.

HENRY   We're just older, Alice. Contrary to popular culture, people do get older.

ALICE   You used to crank the music when you drove.

HENRY   You hated it when I did that.

ALICE   I hate it more that you don't do it anymore.

HENRY   I can't win with you. *(He grabs a pen.)* Here, write it down. Just give me the script. What Henry should say. What Henry should do…

ALICE   Look, it's not that you don't crank the music or dance. It's that you don't even try.

HENRY   I don't want to dance! I never have. It's not a defect of character.

ALICE   We're in a rut, Henry. And we're not doing anything about it.

HENRY   Well trying to fit into some stupidly chic hotel and make it on some very expensive thin sheets will not change us, Alice. We don't fit in here. And the problem is I don't even want to and you do.

          Pause.

ALICE   Maybe that is the problem.

          HENRY tries to comfort ALICE.

HENRY   Look, you know when you go to a dinner party and you walk into the main room and the first thing you see is one of those La-Z-Boy recliners mixed in with some nice furniture? Your first thought is wow, tacky chair. But what's your second thought?

ALICE   Nice drapes?

HENRY   No, I want to sit in that chair. I hope I get that chair. Because it's comfortable and it's going to be a long night, and I want to be comfortable and relaxed and enjoy the party. I want to sit in the recliner. The recliner is good for sitting. A chair should be good for sitting.

ALICE   Oh, God. Please, I'm not a La-Z-Boy recliner in the living room of life. Henry, this is your most insulting metaphor to date. Am I leather at least, or just a bad synthetic? I'm old, worked in, is that it? What the hell are you then, a TV stand, a pool table?

HENRY   No, no, you're not the recliner. We are. Our marriage. We have a comfortable life. We're comfortable together.

ALICE   I can be comfortable with a dog. Comfortable is not passionate.

HENRY   And this is? You say you're here to be passionate and all you've done so far is talk about what's not working. And now you're talking about divorce. It's not exactly a turn-on.

ALICE   I'm telling you how I feel.

HENRY   Well here's a news flash for you, Alice—I know how you feel! You feel disappointed. You feel frustrated. You feel tired. You feel like you're doing all the work. You feel like I'm not good enough for you. And you know what, Alice? I'm starting to feel the same way.

ALICE   Henry...

> *Pause.*

HENRY   Sometimes at night, when I drive up to the house, I just sit in the car. Because I don't want to come in. I don't want to see you. You and the disappointment on your face. I have dreams too, Alice. Desires. Do I make an issue of it? No. What's the point? I can't give in to my disappointment, Alice. Or yours. I have to keep showing up. I may never have a chance to create my Golden Gate Bridge, but I have to appreciate what I have, what we have. If it's not enough for you... maybe you're right.

ALICE   I didn't know that.

HENRY   What?

ALICE   About your Golden Gate Bridge.

HENRY   It's just an example. It's not important.

ALICE   It is important. I want to know stuff, Henry. About you. I'm so bored of "How was your day? Fine." If you're thinking about the girl on the beach even, fine—

HENRY   Alice.

ALICE   No, really. Even if you're thinking about having an affair with her. I understand. I understand why you'd be sick of me.

HENRY   I'm not sick of you.

ALICE   I am.

HENRY   Maybe I do want the girl on the beach sometimes.

ALICE   I understand. She's young. She's beautiful.

HENRY   She's happy.

   Pause. ALICE considers this.

ALICE   *(shrugs)* Happy.

HENRY   You used to laugh all the time. You have the greatest laugh, Alice. And I can hardly remember what it sounds like.

ALICE   Well maybe I need someone to tell me a joke once in a while.

HENRY   Here you go again. Blame me.

ALICE   I'm not blaming you. I'm just saying that you're a part of this. If I'm not happy with us, you're a part of us.

HENRY   I can't make you happy.

ALICE   I don't expect you to make me happy, I just expect that you might be part of the equation. Part of the solution. Involved.

HENRY   We're fine.

ALICE   And is fine good enough for you, Henry?

HENRY   I don't know.

ALICE   You're not even willing to look.

HENRY   I am who I am.

ALICE   You're not. You're not even near to who you are. You're a shadow, Henry.

HENRY   Well it's not your job to change me!

ALICE   Why not? I'm your wife. You're so resistant to change, Henry, to anything new. That's why we're not connecting. You won't try anything because you've got everything all figured out. That's why you didn't get the partnership.

HENRY   What?

ALICE   I know how you can be. You decide how things are. You don't listen. You judge and you criticize but you don't participate anymore. How could you possibly come up with any new ideas like that?

HENRY   I decide how things are? When do I get a chance to have a new idea, for Chrissake? You're the one who decides everything. You say you want me to change, but that would mean you'd have to listen to me, to actually pay attention to me instead of pushing me around like a piece of furniture. You wouldn't know what to do with yourself if I did try something new!

ALICE   That's not true. That's what I want.

HENRY   Like hell you do. You want me to do what you want me to do, and when things don't go the way you like them to you get mad. Or, excuse me—sad.

ALICE   Well I'm not with you at the office, Henry. You lost that partnership all by yourself.

HENRY   (*furious*) You don't know anything about it, Alice!

ALICE   Yes I do, Henry. I know you. Maybe I'm too pushy and controlling, but you know what else I am, Henry? I am your best friend…. And I'm telling you the truth. You're so scared of life—you've forgotten how to live it.

HENRY   And you're here to give me the directions. So, what? So I can become a controlling bitch just like you, Alice?

ALICE   Okay, Henry. You know I'm right and the bottom line is if you're not willing to change, to try something new, to take a chance with us… then I'm not going to do this anymore.

HENRY   Fine. You've got me all figured out. Throw away twenty-five years because you know it all. Fine. Here's a new idea—go fuck yourself!

ALICE   Fine.

HENRY   Fine.

ALICE   I'm taking a bath.

HENRY   FINE.

ALICE   FINE.

> *ALICE grabs her suitcase and exits. HENRY paces the room. He tries to turn on the TV with one of three remotes. He gets muddled with the channels and remote, turning on the TV, music and mood lighting. He hits a music station and can't get it to turn off. The music rises in a frightening composition of techno pop. He frantically pushes at the buttons on the remotes. He tries throwing them on the bed and clapping them off. He finally throws the remotes under the mattress and slams his hand down on the bed, turning the music off, or at least down. Lights up on ALICE in the bathroom, wrapping her hair in a towel. She files her nails, applies cream, etc., as she speaks. HENRY begins to dress and pack his suitcase. The two overlap as they speak in their own spotlights. They each speak in a fluid, overlapping monologue, making one long conversation.*

Goddamn you, Henry!

HENRY   Goddamn you, Alice! Why is it that the things you have no idea, absolutely no idea about, you feel perfectly justified to hold forth on. Like you have any idea what goes on for me at that office. I'd like you to try a day in my life—

ALICE   What was I thinking? Twenty-five years of this. People serve shorter prison sentences. I made a mistake. A terrible mistake I should have made right years ago. I don't need this anymore—

HENRY   This is not what I signed up for, Alice. This is not part of the deal. Work is hard enough.

ALICE   Marriage is a two-way street.

HENRY   Marriage should be easier than this.

ALICE   A marriage takes work.

HENRY   Marriage should be a refuge.

ALICE   Communication.

HENRY   Not a fucking *Oprah Winfrey Show*.

ALICE   I'd be better off on my own.

HENRY   I've had it.

ALICE   Enough is enough.

HENRY   Time to fish or cut bait.

ALICE   A fresh start is what I need.

HENRY   She can have the house.

ALICE   He can have the house.

HENRY   Set me up in an apartment, a room somewhere, I don't care.

ALICE   I'll take the furniture.

HENRY   Just give me my recliner.

ALICE   He can have his recliner.

HENRY   And my remote control.

ALICE   And his TV.

HENRY   Put my feet up with the newspaper.

ALICE   No more newspapers to pick up.

HENRY   An hour of the news. No interruptions.

ALICE   Time for myself.

HENRY   Time to read a book.

ALICE   Time in the garden.

HENRY   Let's see a week minus hours spent arguing, being nagged at, co-operating, discussing our relationship—hell—I could write a book. Maybe I'll take up golf.

ALICE   Maybe I'll get an apartment. Fresh paint. Everything in its place. Where I left it, there when I need it. No more mismatched socks.

HENRY   No more hair in the drain.

ALICE   No more snoring.

HENRY   No more flaxseed oil.

ALICE   No more red meat.

HENRY   No more Oprah.

ALICE   No more *Law and Order*.

HENRY   No more fucking Oprah!

ALICE   I'll read more. I'll read the classics. I'll start a book club. I'll get together with a bunch of smart women; we'll read the classics together. And we'll bring appetizers. Sushi. Henry hates sushi. Perfect.

HENRY   I'll show her. I'll take up a hobby. Forget golf. That's predictable.

ALICE   No, not a book club. I could still meet someone.

HENRY   I'll get a boat. I'll learn how to sail.

ALICE   I'll lose some weight. I'll do yoga. Get flexible. Everybody's so flexible these days. Get my hair cut short. A manicure. And a pedicure. And wax my legs. A facial. A facelift? No. I'll meet someone who loves me for who I am. Sure, there'll be chemistry, a spark. A knowing. We'll know when we see each other the first time at… at a friend's party… a friend who doesn't know Henry…

HENRY   I'll get a cutter. A schooner?

ALICE   …or at a relatives. No, that's awkward… we'll bump into each other at the supermarket… or maybe on a cruise.

HENRY   A sailboat. Take it out. On the sea. Just me and the seagulls. All alone—

> *HENRY and ALICE each have a foot on the bed: their boats. ALICE steps up on the bed/boat as she enjoys her fantasy. HENRY does the same.*

ALICE   On a romantic cruise for singles, older singles… no one under forty… but no one over sixty either… I'll be staring out at the ocean and he'll offer me a glass of champagne. He'll ask me if I'm with someone. I'll demure. Demur? I'll say no. I'll take the champagne. *(She takes the champagne.)* He'll say he likes the cut of my dress because he notices things like that. We'll be comfortable in our silence, watching the sunset together…

> *They both take a big breath, breathing in the salt air.*

HENRY   Yeah, just me and the gulls. No people. No phones ringing.

ALICE   The wind in my hair.

HENRY   No pagers buzzing. No Rich with his cell phone going off like a fucking fanfare.

ALICE   The moon in the sky.

> *HENRY gets off the "boat."*

HENRY   Like it's God calling to say Jesus Christ has resigned and he's the right-hand guy now.

ALICE   His hand on my shoulder?

> *HENRY gets back on the boat.*

HENRY   Nope, none of that out here.

> *ALICE hesitates and steps down.*

ALICE   His hand on my shoulder?

HENRY   Maybe I'll take Alice out on the boat sometime.

ALICE   A divorcee on a cruise. What a cliché.

HENRY   After all, we can still be friends.

ALICE gets up on the boat again.

ALICE   Maybe I'll just say Henry's dead. He died in a tragic boating accident. It's been hard. But I'm strong. The children are grown. Well Jason is only thirteen, but we planned well financially. Henry was very responsible. He looked after us. Sometimes to the exclusion of his own needs, I think maybe—

HENRY   There are memories to talk about.

ALICE   No, I won't talk about Henry. I'll retain an air of mystery.

HENRY   You can't just close the door on twenty-five years.

ALICE   Twenty-five years is a long time.

HENRY and ALICE pause together as if hearing something.

HENRY   But you can't live in the past.

HENRY gets off the boat for good. He zips up his suitcase and grabs his keys and wallet to leave.

ALICE   It was a wonderful life—

HENRY   You have to shut the door sometime.

ALICE   And now I'm getting on with it.

HENRY   I'm not dead yet.

ALICE   There's a whole future ahead of us.

ALICE and HENRY face each other, still in their own worlds.

Me, I mean.

The moment breaks as ALICE reaches for her suitcase and exits to the bathroom. The lights change back to room light as HENRY picks up his suitcase. He heads for the door. He's just about out the door when he pauses, catching the reflection of himself leaving in the mirror. He puts the suitcase down. He feels the extra roll of fat on his stomach. He looks at his hairline. He sees himself and turns back into the room, unsettled. He sits down on the bed, unwittingly activating the remote underneath him. The Rolling Stones' "Miss You" filters in. He takes the remote from under the mattress. He moves to turn the music off and then hesitates, listening to the music. In this moment HENRY makes a decision. Mustering all his will, he attempts a dance step, tentatively putting one foot out and then quickly pulling it back in. He stops. He tries another. And one more. HENRY, very slowly and stiffly begins to dance. First tentatively, and then, as the music overtakes him in full abandon, combining a series of dance moves that spans many decades. He dances à la HENRY, purposefully, then joyfully. Mid-dance he grabs the phone, turning the music down with the remote to speak.

HENRY Hello? This is two nineteen. Yes, two nineteen. No, no. The towels are fine. I'd like to order a bottle of champagne. Uh, well what do you have? Uh-huh. Just give me a good bottle. How much is that? Jesus. How about a pretty good bottle? Okay. And two glasses. Chilled. And wait, can you put a flower or something on the tray. A rose, yes, a rose.

HENRY hangs up the phone. He picks up the remote and turns the music back on. Now HENRY is in his fantasy dance: a full blowout club dance on the bed with accompanying lights. In the middle of HENRY'S air guitar, ALICE appears in the doorway wearing black sunglasses, a leather trench coat, black slip and stockings underneath, and high heels: dominatrix gear à la ALICE. She strikes a pose and watches HENRY dance. He doesn't see her. She picks up the remote and switches off the music. She goes back to her pose. The lights return to normal. HENRY jumps off the bed, rushing to cover up his dancing. He still doesn't look at ALICE.

ALICE   Hi.

HENRY   *(caught)* I was…

ALICE   You were dancing.

HENRY   I was just fooling around.

ALICE   You're a naughty boy.

          HENRY turns to see ALICE in her gear.

HENRY   What?

ALICE   You've been a very bad boy.

          ALICE cracks her whip.

          Get on the bed.

HENRY   Alice! What? Where did you—

ALICE   Get on the bed.

          HENRY backs up onto the bed. ALICE takes a few tentative steps toward him on her very high heels. She wraps the whip around his neck.

          You want to sit in a La-Z-Boy recliner, or do you want to feel some real leather against your skin?

HENRY   Alice…

          ALICE runs her leather whip down the side of HENRY's leg.

ALICE   Are you surprised?

HENRY   I didn't expect this from you.

          ALICE moves around the room, enjoying her freedom, but a little wobbly on the shoes and with the whip.

ALICE   Exactly! Let's get physical.

HENRY   Physical?

ALICE	I can be wild, Henry. *(She snorts from the aromatherapy.)*
HENRY	Where did you get this stuff?
ALICE	I have contacts, Henry. I'm not just a wife. I am a sexual being too.
HENRY	A sexual being.
ALICE	You don't think I'm sexy?
HENRY	I just don't think of you in this way.

> *ALICE takes off her trench coat revealing a slip and garters underneath.*

ALICE	Well maybe you should. There is more to me than meets the eye.
HENRY	I can see that, Alice.
ALICE	I am a woman, Henry.
HENRY	I know that.

> *She gets on the bed. Walking around him. HENRY is a little afraid of what she's going to do with the whip.*

ALICE	I am a woman. Mother, friend, wife, real estate agent— but woman first.
HENRY	I hear you, Helen Reddy.
ALICE	*(cracking the whip)* So roll over, bitch.

> *HENRY rolls over.*

HENRY	You're not going to hit me with that thing are you?

> *ALICE pulls off her sunglasses and reassuringly shows him the whip.*

ALICE	What? No. It's a prop. It's supposed to be sexy.
HENRY	Oh, okay.

> *ALICE gets back into character, twirling the whip in a lasso above her head.*

ALICE	We're going to get naughty now.

HENRY   Naughty? Naughty!

ALICE   Yeah, uh… do you want me to talk dirty to you?

HENRY   Well no, not really… do you know how to talk dirty?

> *ALICE thinks about it for a second and then gets into a position to talk dirty but has trouble finding the words.*

ALICE   Umm… I'm going to come over there and lick… I'm going to take your… wait till I… *(She gives up.)*

HENRY   I know. Try a metaphor.

ALICE   What?

HENRY   You know, like… you're going to come over here and peel my banana—

ALICE   Oh! Okay, good… good. Got it. I'm going to come over there and take your pumpkin… tomatoes? Ahh… cucumber!

HENRY   *(HENRY snaps his fingers.)* Cucumber's good.

ALICE   …and mix it with yogurt, and we're going to make some tzatziki together…

HENRY   *(puzzled)* Tzatziki?

> *ALICE cracks her whip, waving her butt in HENRY's face.*

ALICE   Don't you want to play with my pita, Henry?

HENRY   Sure, I…

ALICE   You got a little feta for me, big guy?

HENRY   I'm not sure this whole Greek thing…

ALICE   Yeah. Maybe I should just say dirty words.

HENRY   *(unsure)* Okay. If you want to.

ALICE   Okay ah… fuck. *(cracks her whip)*

> *ALICE moves around the room, riffing on the word "fuck." She says it loudly and softly, cracking her whip,*

repeating it quickly and elongating the word, trying to make it work for her and HENRY. She enjoys it at first as HENRY kindly cheers her on, but as she loses fire she catches a glimpse of herself in the mirror and the "fucks" become more difficult to say, sadder and softer until finally it's not about HENRY anymore, but about ALICE and her disappointment in herself. She flails with the whip a few times before letting out one last, frustrated fuck and bursts into tears. HENRY watches her from the bed, not sure what to do as his wife falls apart.

Fuck! Fuck. *(a riff on as many fucks as needed to help ALICE fall apart)* Oh, fuck. What am I doing, Henry? Oh God, I was wrong, Henry. It's not you, I don't know anymore, it's me. Look at me. What am I doing? This isn't…. What's happened to me? Where did I go? I never used to care how you chewed. I used to be happy.

HENRY places his robe over ALICE's shoulders as he gently sits her down on the bed.

Allan Morgan and Susinn McFarlane
photo by: David Cooper

Do you remember how I used to be? How we used to be? Remember when we didn't care if we got enough sleep? Remember getting stoned?

They sit on the bed staring forward, quietly remembering.

HENRY   Hot knives.

ALICE   Tequila and gala kegs.

HENRY   God, the hangovers.

ALICE   An Aspirin and a Bloody Mary.

HENRY   Reading the paper Sunday mornings. Those weird slippers you wore.

ALICE   I painted the house in them.

HENRY   Four days.

ALICE   Right before Nicky was born.

HENRY   Goodbye Sunday mornings.

ALICE   In bed with us.

HENRY   The three of us.

ALICE   Then four.

HENRY / ALICE
                     Then Jason.

ALICE   Surprise.

HENRY   Bulldozers…

ALICE   …dump trucks…

HENRY   …front-end loaders…

ALICE   And the trips we took.

HENRY   When we were young. Remember young?

ALICE   Mexico.

HENRY   Oregon.

ALICE   And Hawaii. Remember Hawaii? The picnics we had on the— *(She stops.)*

HENRY   On the beach.

ALICE   Tell me your fantasy, Henry.

HENRY   She wears a green dress. The dress slips off her shoulder as she places the picnic on the blanket... I can see the outline of her breast as she reaches for a plate of...

ALICE   Strawberries.

HENRY   I kiss her and we both taste like strawberries. I feel the warm sand in my toes as she lies beside me. In a moment I turn to her, pulled, because there is nothing else I could possibly do at this moment than take this girl, this woman, into my arms and make love to her. We are without words. I open my eyes and I see blue sky, blue sky that goes on forever, that will never end.

                HENRY kisses ALICE.

ALICE   And the sound of waves.

HENRY   The sound of waves.

ALICE   And the smell of strawberries.

HENRY   Yes.

ALICE   Crushed into my dress. My green dress.

HENRY   Yes.

                ALICE meets HENRY's gaze. She is deeply moved.

ALICE   I'm not that girl anymore.

                HENRY speaks quietly.

HENRY   When you're folding the laundry.

ALICE   What?

HENRY   The way you bend to reach into the hamper. The way you give everything a quick shake. The way your hair falls in your eyes. Your concentration. The way you smooth each piece with your hands. Each piece. It's sexy. You're sexy.

ALICE   I fold the laundry a lot.

HENRY   You do.

> *They turn to each other after a moment. ALICE kisses HENRY gently. HENRY kisses her more passionately. ALICE reaches for him but HENRY pulls away a little.*

I'm not...

ALICE   What's wrong, Henry?

HENRY   Nothing, I...

ALICE   Is it me?

HENRY   It's not you.

ALICE   *(gently)* It doesn't have to be fast, Henry.

HENRY   It's not...

ALICE   We can take it slow.

HENRY   It's not sex.

ALICE   What is it, Henry?

HENRY   I just... I haven't felt like—

> *The doorbell rings, stopping HENRY. He gets up to answer it.*

ALICE   Tell me.

> *HENRY turns to ALICE.*

HENRY   I haven't felt like me for a long time, Alice. How did it happen? When did I stop having new ideas and start having a conservative sensibility?

> *HENRY goes offstage for the champagne. He brings it in and stands waiting for ALICE'S response.*

ALICE   *(delighted)* Henry.

HENRY puts down the tray and picks up the two glasses, clicking them together.

HENRY   *(flatly)* They're goddamn plastic.

Pause.

ALICE   *(afraid)* What?

HENRY   *(laughs)* The glasses are plastic. Plastic!

ALICE   *(laughing)* I miss you so much, Henry.

HENRY   Me too, Alice.

HENRY pops the champagne and shows the bottle to ALICE.

It's a pretty good bottle.

ALICE   Come make a toast to your old time-share over here.

HENRY pours it into the plastic glasses. He holds one up for a toast, facing his wife.

Allan Morgan and Susinn McFarlane
photo by: David Cooper

HENRY   When you first visit a place you always wanted to visit it's exciting. New. It takes your breath away. And then because it's so wonderful you visit it again and again. And it isn't new anymore. But you come to really know it. And because you love it so much you come to live there. Do you know what you call a place that you love so much that you come to live there? Home. *(His voice catches.)* You call it home, Alice.

ALICE raises her glass.

ALICE   Hail Caesar.

HENRY   Hail Caesar.

They toast.

Lights fade to black.